Notes from Gusto:

Relationship Reminders

Elizabeth Day

BR

Blue Root Press

For Toph

Introduction

You've earned badge after stripe after award in the relation-ship department, simply by engaging with other people as you have, with intensity and earnest hope and the generos-ity of sharing who you are. The relationship reminders that follow are triggers to help you tap into what you've already experienced in your life and the wisdom you've gained from those interactions. They're specific ways to think about and approach your relationships, taken out of context and set in black and white for you to point to, hold on to, and come back to. So that you always remember.

As you well know, relationships require patience, a desire to understand someone else, and a willingness to share your-self. They take time—in fact, as much as you're willing to give. They beg for honesty, especially when it's most difficult and no relationship goes past any starting or re-starting line without an incredible amount of courage on your part.

Relationships are full of layers that require a willingness to both give and receive. They require a constant flexibility and the wisdom to know when it's time to push forward or to let go, to forgive or to be forgiven, to stand up or to back down. They bring out your vulnerability and tap at the most fragile aspects of your character, and yet they bring out your greatest strengths and the hero in you. They require an assertion of who you are and at the same time an openness to discovering what you didn't realize about you.

Relationships aren't always easy, even the best of the best, and they take a lot of work. So for every relationship you're in— and realize how many there are—be immensely proud. They're the most generous and important roles you've ever chosen to take on.

Keep on shining.

An unwavering fan of you,

~ Gusto

Suggestions for How to Use this Book

Daily Focus
Begin each day by reading one of the notes—either in order or out of order, whichever feels right to you—and use the message as your focus point during the day as you live out your relationships and leave your mark.

An Invitation to Answers
Think of a question you've been struggling with or wondering about. Write it down or say it aloud and then let it go. Take a few deep breaths. Relaxed and trusting your instinct, choose a "random" page and read the message. Consider it in relation to the question you posed. Sit with it. Let it simmer.

Conversation Topic
Pick a note. Then invite someone or a group of people to discuss it with you. Take a walk, sit down to a meal, or strike up an unplanned conversation, and see where the message in the note takes you.

Journal/Diary Prompt
Choose a note and use it as a starting point to write about

your relationship. When you're done writing, revel in your ability to free yourself through uncensored expression, and recognize all the wisdom and answers you have within you.

Art Muse
Choose a note and allow it to inspire an art piece—one of a kind, created by you, with whatever medium you're moved to use. When you're done, celebrate the artist in you.

Ready Reading
Leave the book somewhere where you'll pass it often so that you can pick it up, turn to a page, and focus your attention on the relationship that matters most to you in that moment.

1.

When you don't quite feel like yourself, like there's a disconnect between the you who's talking to someone and the real you, and you want to feel like you again...

When you're talking to someone but feel a wall between you two, and you want to feel more connected...

There's a surefire way to break through that barrier between you and yourself, or between you and someone else: take a deep breath, tap into the wildly active yet calming love inside you, and tell your truth—about anything and everything.

Raw honesty, spoken with love, has an astounding power.

2.

There's nothing your strength can't take on,
nothing your sense of humor can't disarm,
and nothing your self-love can't handle.

Remember that.

3.

Express how you feel.

   Sometimes your words might come out
scratchy, like an old record – no problem.
And if at times you feel like a broken record,
that's fine too; sometimes it takes a while to
be heard.

   More often than you'll know, when you
express how you feel, no matter how it sounds
to you, it's music to someone's ears.

4.

When you're completely honest with yourself, what you've known all along suddenly becomes apparent, and what you don't know isn't intimidating anymore.

Honesty allows you to name each emotion you're feeling, and then to recognize that no feeling is too big to handle or too small to matter.

Turn on the light. See what there is to see. No matter what you find yourself looking at, you'll eventually be face-to-face with relief and clarity.

5.

Keep telling yourself what you need to hear, because it doesn't get more powerful or effective than coming straight from you.

First and foremost, you listen to you.

6.

Next time you're tempted to quickly muscle your way through a conversation, to get the results you want from it or to get it over with, try doing the opposite.

Slow down and relax into it, at ease as you consciously move through it, as if you have all the time in the world and there's nothing that matters more than what you're engaging in this very moment.

When you relax, you become receptive to your own inner wisdom. Your heart opens. Your mind opens. Your creativity and resourcefulness open. Which then opens the space for significant and meaningful progress... and for you to find your greatest strengths.

7.

Questions asked of the caterpillar about how long it'll be staying in that dark, confining cocoon, and—does it really like it in there? These make the caterpillar feel like maybe there's something wrong with being there, and the caterpillar begins feeling a loneliness it hadn't felt before. It begins to wonder, *Is there something wrong with me? Am I stuck? Is this bad where I am?* And it doesn't need to be told, "I wish you'd just come out of there," because if it could, if it knew how, it would. It's just not time yet.

The butterfly, having been there before, knows this. And that's why it gives no attention to the obvious things most others notice about the caterpillar. Instead, the butterfly whispers through the walls of the cocoon to the caterpillar, "This will pass, I promise. You'll have wings with mesmerizing colors and riveting patterns... I can picture them! Oh... look at you! A free spirit with no constraints, you're dancing, twirling, and gliding... Oh my... Yes! But for now, feel however you feel. It's okay. Where you are right now is important. Soon, my friend, you'll be flying free." It's the unconditional love and confidence in the caterpillar that turn it into a butterfly and bring it out of its cocoon.

8.

Never let possible consequences stop you from standing up for yourself. In fact, the only consequences you ever need to concern yourself with are those that would result from you not standing up for yourself.

9.

The people in your life, their quirks and weaknesses and faults and the far majority of their mistakes—they're not about you, and they don't say anything about you. They have nothing to do with you. They're part of that person's own personal story, nothing beyond that. And so the question of forgiveness becomes a moot point. How can there be anything you need to forgive when, at the core level, it has nothing to do with you?

Don't create pain where there's no need for it. Those moments don't call for forgiveness; they call for strength or compassion or clarity, sometimes all three. Forgive your own quirks and weaknesses and faults and mistakes, and you'll free yourself of any attachment to anyone else's. Forgive yourself, and you'll find it easy to be wildly generous in your tolerance of others' imperfections. Forgive yourself, and when you take notice of quirks and weaknesses and faults and mistakes, yours or other people's, it will be a different experience entirely, one shaped by strength or compassion or clarity, one that's downright as humanly beautiful as it gets.

10.

People need to hear what you have to say.

Be bold. Be honest. Be you.

But always—always—come from a place of radiant love, recognizing when you're not there yet and waiting until you are.

It's the beginning of countless "best things that ever happened."

11.

If you were to disconnect for a moment from all the labels used to describe the many roles you play in other people's lives, you know what you'd find?

You.

Disconnect, just for a moment. Until... there's only you, who you are, separate from everyone else.

Because it's really good to remember.

12.

Be incredibly kind to yourself,
showing true understanding.

No matter what, no exceptions.

It'll shift every relationship you have
for the better.

13.

Something not quite at its best, with some flaws here and a few cracks there, can still be beautiful. Sometimes that's easy to see. And sometimes, in order to see it, it takes a willingness to look at it from a perspective you're not used to.

Shift angles. Stand back.

The more you look, the more peace you get from realizing that not everything needs to be fixed or changed.

14.

Imagine yourself in a conversation with the first person who comes to mind right now...

And consider this: possibilities expand and what you most want becomes possible in a whole new way when, while interacting with someone, you free yourself of the need to be right.

15.

You can play your own tune and still be part of a cohesive duo, trio, and plenty more. In fact, the most powerful rhythms are born from the combination of individual instruments and distinctly different notes.

Hold onto your you-ness, celebrating what your individuality brings to your relationships.

16.

When it's your turn to listen, being a good listener—a really good listener—
can change someone's life.

And when it's your turn to talk, being authentic and courageously sticking to your truth can change a life, too.

Sometimes yours, sometimes theirs.

17.

You always have the choice to engage—or not. It's an energetic doing you have complete control over no matter the circumstances.

When you give your energy to certain people, it makes you feel good. In fact, it makes you feel more like you. In those cases, engage, engage, engage—with all the energy you've got.

With others, that may not be the case. Engaging makes you feel less like you. There's a toxicity, or the timing's off, or... don't worry about the reason. Just detach for now. Simply detach and pull your energy back.

Whether you choose to engage or disengage, the decision is as powerful as it is simple.

18.

The closer you are to someone, and the more integral a part of any group you are, the more important it is to recognize and honor your individuality. When you've forgotten that or are having a hard time seeing it, it helps to place yourself at the center again, the hub of the wheel.

At the same time, it's just as important to recognize that even though you're an individual, you're also part of something bigger. When you've forgotten that, it helps to see yourself as one of the integral spokes on the wheel.

You'll know you've found the perfect balance when getting the wheel to turn feels effortless, and you take yourself where you truly want to go.

19.

Make a conscious effort to be yourself.

No matter where you are, regardless of what you're doing, and with zero dependence on who you're with.

The more you're yourself, the more interesting your life is, the further your energy goes, the easier your decisions are, and the clearer your voice is.

Everything just becomes simpler. And better.

20.

As often as you can, mean what you say
rather than trying to explain
what you mean.

The more complicated it is,
the simpler you can make it.

21.

When things get really uncomfortable in a relationship because it's sad or confusing, or because you're feeling angry or frustrated or afraid, it can be tempting to look for a quick fix, to cover the whole thing with a Band-Aid or to settle for a good-enough-for-now solution.

Don't.

Because now is what you have. Now is everything that matters.

Instead, sit in the uncomfortable-ness until there is no more discomfort. Feel. Think. Cry. Laugh. Yell. Whisper. Write. Sing. Dance. Walk. Run. Draw. Sit still. Do whatever it takes until you're no longer sad or angry or confused or frustrated or afraid. Sit with it for a minute, an hour, days, however long it takes, so that when you're through with it, you're really all the way through it.

Nothing is as exhilarating as standing up from that uncomfortable chair and being able to thank it and walk away from it, knowing it's no longer yours to sit in, while being so grateful that you did.

22.

Let your guard down and play.

23.

Because love is much more powerful and determined than it is simple or black and white, it sometimes leaves an invisible scar as it etches itself into your experiences.

When that's the case, be proud. It's an extraordinary type of scar, one that can be earned only from living fearlessly and feeling deeply; it's an absolutely sure sign of a remarkable and exceptional life being lived.

Keep on loving.

24.

Don't worry about what it sounds like, what it looks like, or how it might be perceived.

Ask yourself just one question: am I being me?

Feel the thrill that comes from the answer being yes, and enjoy how wide and far-reaching the reverberations of authenticity are.

25.

You can have what you want, and
so can everyone else; there are always ways,
and there's always plenty.

Let that thought simmer...

and see what eventually bubbles up
with its song to you.

26.

Forgive the imperfections.

All of them.

Starting with the ones that have been
bothering you the most.

Forgive them deeply and generously.

27.

You don't always have to search far and wide,
crossing wild seas and climbing the tallest of
mountains to find what you're looking for.

Sometimes it's right there in front of you,
embedded in what you already have.

What a surprise it can be when you're open
to seeing it.

28.

Love is rarely perfect. And sometimes it can leave you feeling a little chiseled. But you always get to decide how it will shape you.

Will it give you rough edges?

Or round you out?

Or perhaps it will shape you into more of who you are.

It's up to you. Always.

29.

Love fearlessly, without regrets.

30.

Think of yourself the way you want them to think of you.

Give yourself what you want them to give you.

Tell yourself what you want them to tell you.

You'll end up having a lot to think about, much more to give, and a whole lot more to say, because when you love yourself the way you want other people to love you, you need nothing except to give love away.

31.

Something happens when you look at someone and, for whatever reason, decide in that moment that they don't need to change anything about them. In fact, you genuinely hope they never do.

In that moment, when you're looking at them, not saying anything, just arriving at that clarity, stress dissolves, weights lift themselves up and off and put themselves down, and an undeniable excitement kicks in. No wonder you always end up smiling.

32.

When you start to look at how much you have in common with the person you're most challenged by, with the one you just don't "get," it dramatically shifts how you see yourself, how you see them, and therefore how you interact.

Look with gentle eyes. There's so much to see.

When you find all there is to like and all that connects you, you have a lot more fun, you're a lot more productive, and you end up with a deeper sense of both self and belonging.

33.

The reason self-love is so important is because it's the transparent and unconditional permission you give yourself to love your life and the person living it.

When you say yes to it and allow it to be your navigator, you find yourself either loving what you're doing or doing more of what you love to do, and you find yourself loving the people you're surrounded by even more, or instead surrounding yourself more and more by the people you love.

Love you and see where it takes you.

34.

You can get so used to seeing the weeds in a garden that you don't even notice them anymore. It's the same with energy-draining thoughts about a relationship; you may be so used to thinking something that you don't even realize that thought is there.

Like weeds shadowing the flowers that are trying to bloom, negative thoughts can crowd out the positive ones. In fact, once you start pulling out the weeds and getting rid of them, you're likely to find stunning blooms that you didn't even know were there.

Weed your garden of thoughts, and you'll see immediate results in your relationships. Getting rid of even just one energy-draining thought will change the look of everything.

35.

In any given moment, the bond connecting
you to anyone or anything is as weak or
strong as you decide it is.

36.

Who tugs at the adventurer in you and—while acknowledging that there are indeed dark clouds above—gently dares you to look directly at the sun?

Who's as excited about learning more about you—the real you—as they are about knowing themselves?

If you were to take a leap of faith, who is the net that will always be there, ready to catch you but promising you won't need them to?

It's good to know.

37.

Letting go changes the dynamic
—every time—
loosening what's been too tight.

Now, there is space. And now,
anything is possible.

38.

You don't have to worry about
what anyone else thinks.

Because what you think is always
the starting point from which
everything else follows.

39.

It's not possible to overestimate the importance of loving yourself. You see, until you do, it makes it difficult to recognize all the love that's standing right on your doorstep. It can knock and knock and knock, but still...

On the flip side, when you decide to love yourself, it's easy to see and hear the love trying to find its way to you. And it's easy to open the door and let it in and welcome it... because you understand why it's there.

Love yourself: One thought at a time. One belief at a time. One action at a time.

40.

You're not them. And they're not you. So instead of comparing, focus your energy on being you.

Get into it. Get down to it.

You're not limited by anyone else's experiences, anyone else's beliefs, or anyone else's projections on you or assumptions about you.

You know who you are—so be that person—because the surest way to find your true path and tap into your bliss every single day is to be authentically you.

41.

When you decide to consciously and deliberately love someone — anyone — you shift your entire world. In that instant, you become the most powerful and influential person in your life.

   Deciding to love above all else changes the words you use with people, your approach, your intentions, and your actions. Which then ends up dramatically changing the results.

42.

The more you focus on the things in your life
that make you feel happy and confident and
strong, the less time and space there is for
things that make you feel anything else.

Dwell with purpose.

43.

Find out—again and again—what happens when you remember that everyone's doing their best and is still learning, still figuring it out.

Each person, in his or her own way, is intimately familiar with what it feels like to be on unsure feet, sometimes needing to try hard in order to simply stay standing.

44.

It's liberating to accept that you can't control what anyone thinks of you or how someone interacts with you.

And when you think about it a little more and realize that you wouldn't want to control that—ever, with anyone—a peace like no other settles within you.

And then, when you take it a step further and remember that what you do have complete control over, always, whether it's someone you've known for your whole life or someone you're coming across for the first time today, is what you think of them and how you interact with them—that's when the excitement really begins to build.

There is no power equal to your right and ability to define your relationship with another person, no matter who it is, which can quickly translate into an ordinary moment becoming an extraordinary one.

45.

When you realize that there's absolutely
nothing you need to change about you,
everything begins to make complete sense.

Things get simpler, and you start to
recognize perfection as nothing more than an
unnecessary and distracting complication. You
stop looking for it in yourself and in other
people. You stop waiting for it to show up,
realizing you don't need it to.

And everything gets a lot more fun.

46.

You've got so much love to give. A staggering amount, really.

So it's no wonder that when you give it away, without expectation, without counting or comparing, realizing it's yours to give unconditionally and even recklessly, understanding that you need no permission to do it... it's no wonder that that's when your spark is at its brightest and there's a contagious happiness about you that can't be explained or contained.

Keep loving like it's the most important job you have.

47.

In every relationship, remind yourself often: *I don't have to. I get to.*

It always looks and feels so different after that.

48.

Needing anything from others that you have no control over receiving—things like validation, praise, gratitude, acceptance, encouragement, and attention—drains your energy and leaves you feeling powerless. When you realize, however, that it's a choice to need those things, you can choose to let any one of those needs go. It's no more complicated than flipping a switch: You used to need it. Now you don't.

Try it. Experiment with it.

I could tell you what I know, that you'll experience a freedom you've never had before, empowerment that keeps building on itself, a dramatic increase in confidence, a new perspective on everyone in your life, and that you'll immediately love yourself more deeply than you ever have, but nothing I can say even comes close to capturing the cosmic distance between before flipping the switch and after.

You're not needy. You never have been. And now you get to know it and feel it.

49.

Feel it like you once did.

Close your eyes.

Go back.

Remember.

See how it changes everything.

50.

If something's not working for you—if it's not making you feel how you want to feel—it's okay. Just acknowledge it. Move past that resistance to overlook it or ignore it or pretend that it isn't so. Resistance makes it so much bigger than it actually is.

Just tell your truth.

Once you acknowledge that something isn't working for you, you move out of its brokenness. Now you're in a space where you can look at it from a distance, and when you do so... you'll know exactly what to do.

You have so many answers inside you waiting to come out. As soon as you admit there's a question, you give permission to the answer to surface.

51.

Their story is theirs.

And yours is yours.

Deliberately choose not to mix up the two.

52.

If someone's struggling with a sadness they're ready to move on from, and you want to help them, visualize their heart filled with a contagious joy. And hold that vision of them, no matter what.

If it's an old anger they're struggling with, visualize them filled with a peace and calm that emanates from their core. And hold that vision of them, no matter what.

When the struggle is physical pain, picture them perfectly healthy. And hold that vision of them, no matter what.

When it's finding a purpose they're struggling with, picture them feeling fulfilled and full of excitement about their life. And hold that vision of them, no matter what.

If it's fear that's the struggle, visualize them as fearless, filled with indestructible trust. And hold that vision of them, no matter what.

When low self-esteem is the struggle, visualize them sporting pride and fully warranted confidence. And hold that vision of them, no matter what.

The same goes for you—when you're the one who's struggling and you want to help yourself.

Experience the power of your vision.

53.

Let go...
And keep letting go, until
you feel noticeably lighter.

That's how you create the space
for something far better than what
you were holding tightly to.

54.

Whenever you want to, and as often as you want to, you can focus on whatever it is that makes you think to yourself, *I might actually be the luckiest person in the world.* No matter where you are. No matter what you're doing.

You don't have to tell anyone why you suddenly can't stop smiling. But you should know: your life-is-good vibe is wildly contagious. In fact, you might notice people giving you a second look... and then a third. And then they might actually make excuses to be around you.

55.

Whether you're giving space to another person
or yourself, make sure it's at the very least
a calm, neutral space. You can go so far as
to give it a positive, trusting, enthusiastic
space, but avoid giving resentment-filled
space because that kind of space isn't much
space at all.

   True space opens all the doors and windows,
letting plenty of air in and out so that
everyone can breathe fully and deeply...
and relax.

56.

When you're inclined to do so, be open
to changing direction and to altering your
destination. Open up to changing your mind
and to altering even long-held opinions.
Be willing to change your approach and
alter your perception.

It can be done without changing, even
a little bit, who you are. In fact, it's
how you discover a lot more of who you are.

57.

Sometimes the solution is to simply let go.

If ever you're in a tug-of-war that's taking you nowhere, you always have the choice to simply let go of your end of the rope.

Just let it go.

And since you will no longer be fiercely holding on, you can shake your hands out, spread your arms wide, and bask in your freedom.

58.

How do you want to feel?

No matter where you are, what you're doing, or who's standing next to you, remember how you want to feel. Let it be the center, the trunk, its implications extending in every direction, like branches that tango, mingle, dip down, stretch up, tiptoe out, and reach around.

When you know how you want to feel, you usually end up choosing to feel that way too.

59.

Love is made of an endless list of likes.

60.

Take the time to first process your thoughts
and feelings on your own, even if it means
stepping out of your routine to do so.

   Especially if it means stepping out of your
routine to do so.

61.

You do know what you're doing.

That's where that surge of confidence
that sometimes shows up out of the blue
comes from.

It's why, on a very deep level, there's a part
of you that has never worried
and never will.

62.

Be nice.

Explore what that means when applied
to him.

Discover what it looks like in consideration of
her.

Find out what being nice means in relation to
you.

63.

When something isn't going the way you want it
to, particularly when someone else is involved,
by detaching for a moment and deciding "it
might be okay," you open the space for seeing
it from a different perspective and eventually
feeling more than just okay about it.

And immediately, you feel way more than just
okay about you.

64.

The more freely you speak, the more intently and thought-fully you listen. This is why: because once you take a good look inside yourself and let those words out, it's much easier to look outside yourself and let those words in. And then pretty much anything is possible.

65.

Be fair.

66.

It's so much easier to get clear and into
a place of empowerment when you give zero
attention to thoughts that begin with "If only
they would" or "They should" and instead focus
on thoughts that begin with "I can," exploring
your many choices.

When you quiet the negativity, you can hear
the possibility.

67.

People notice it when you're five times nicer
than you need to be and ten times nicer than
you feel like being. And that's when they
think of you as a hero.

68.

The more you fall in love with yourself, the more you'll fall in love with your life and all the other people in it.

And the less you'll pay attention to the things that have no place in that love fest.

69.

You don't need to wait around for someone
else to call the shots.

70.

When you miss someone, let yourself miss them.

Feel it fully.

Because whether the person you miss is five feet away from you or five hundred miles, it opens a channel between you two. When you feel yourself missing them, you're actually sending all the love you have for them directly through that channel. They may not know who's sending it, but they'll feel that surge of love coming their way. And who knows? It just might be exactly what they needed.

71.

Alone time is crucial. Even just five minutes. Just you.

Think alone. Feel on your own. First.

What do you really think?

How do you really feel?

Hear the answers. Allow them. Free them. It's between you and yourself. It's rewarding, energizing, positively liberating. And you'll wonder why you even hesitated to think on your own first, to feel on your own first, and you'll promise yourself to do it again, every day, all the time.

Because once you think on your own first, and feel on your own first, then you know a lot more than you did.

72.

It's the absence of any agenda except to positively "add to" in one way or another that draws people to you.

73.

Next time you want someone to be more open, less judgmental, more attentive, more or less of anything, first do it yourself for three days — the more or less — particularly with that person.

After three days, one of two things is likely to happen. Either you'll be in a much different place when asking for them to consider being more or less of something, or your need for them to be any different will have dissolved.

74.

Sometimes things are heavy. Carry them for a while when the other person can't.

75.

Never underestimate the strength of your
positive energy and your positive thoughts.

You make the impossible possible.

76.

You instinctively know when to take a few steps back, whether it's physically, emotionally, or energetically, and whether it's for five minutes or five days. In doing so, you disengage from any back-and-forth, allowing whatever it is to simmer for a little while, to be what it is, to be acted upon by its own energy.

And in the meantime, in the space you're giving yourself, you too get to simmer for a little while, letting things be as they are, allowing for forces invisible to the naked eye to do their thing.

And then, when you re-engage, knowing it's time, you'll see it all, including yourself, in a whole new light.

77.

Be kinder than necessary.

78.

In order to make sure you're not getting lost
in the shuffle, once in a while you need to
take the deck of cards, shuffle it yourself,
and then deal your own hand.

79.

In order to be clear about how you feel, you sometimes need to distinguish between what you actually feel and how you think you should feel.

The difference between the two is sometimes a valley apart. And it's in that middle, caught between the two, where confusion can take hold.

When you recognize what it is you actually feel and let go of any and every "should," you easily find yourself up out of the deep valley of confusion, firmly standing on one side, clearly recognizing every "should" feeling on the other side as simply not true for you.

And as soon as you're clear about how you feel, what to do next becomes obvious.

80.

Just as each person you interact with, no matter what type of interaction it is and no matter how long it lasts, has an effect on you, you too have an effect on other people. Whatever the nature of the effect, it's specific. And real.

It's a choice you make, whether by choosing deliberately or by defaulting to whatever mood you happen to be in, letting it be the decider.

So, you interact with someone. You talk to them, or you think about them, or you look at them. And the effect takes place.

The question is: what effect do you want to have on other people?

Here's why it matters: because you matter. A lot.

81.

No matter how good you are at reading people, it's impossible to know for sure what they're thinking. Unless you ask them.

And no matter how good you are at discerning people's moods, it's impossible to know for sure how they're feeling. Unless you ask them.

On the flip side, no matter how familiar someone is with you, they can't know for sure what you're thinking or feeling. Unless you tell them.

82.

"I love you."
Sometimes that's all that needs to be said.
With or without words.

83.

You have to remember who you are in order to be who you are. So how do you remember?

You remember by recognizing fear when it knocks on the door and saying, "No, that's not who I am," choosing not to let it in. You return to being your fearless self, someone who implicitly trusts their life.

You remember by speaking your truth, even when it's difficult, because nothing brings about clarity and a true sense of self like raw honesty.

You remember by not worrying about what other people think of you and instead listening to what you think, because the voice inside you has never forgotten who you are.

You remember by being willing to feel what you feel because your feelings, when fully felt, will eventually guide you to say what needs to be said and do what needs to be done in order to reach your destinies.

You remember by doing the things you love to do because they're a powerful expression of who you are. They're lamp-posts on your journey, there to lead the way.

The reason you're here is to be who you are, which is why being who you are feels so good, so right, so purpose-filled and meaningful.

84.

You never need anyone's permission to love
them. And the timing is always perfect,
and the circumstances are always right.

85.

If you're not happy with how it's going, you can start all over anytime you want to, no matter what it is.

Throw the full spirit of you into it, not holding back and not forcing yourself forward, just being who you are right now at this point.

86.

Lightly but deliberately hold on to what's
yours, and freely but with gratitude let go
of what is not.

To determine which is which, ask yourself,
"Is _____ about me or what I'm about?"
If the answer is yes, it's yours. If the
answer is no, it's not.

87.

In every relationship you have, there are two separate individuals: you and the other person. You're not them, and they're not you. Remember that. Hold on to it.

At times, you'll be on different pages, and at times you'll think in ways that are worlds apart. You'll both have feelings that are all your own, opinions that differ, perspectives that come from a place that isn't shared. Allow it, embrace it, and decide to be more than just okay with it. Be confident in the differences. Celebrate them.

Create a kind space for individuality because the purpose of two people being connected in any way is not to make either person into someone they are not, but instead, through the togetherness, to bring out more of who each person is.

88.

Rather than wondering, worrying,
or guessing...

Just ask.

89.

Blaming someone else or a circumstance for your mood or actions suggests that you're a puppet, and you're no such thing.

You're in control of your demeanor and moves. You have no strings that have to be pulled, and you're never at the mercy of anyone or anything, because you're always fully empowered by your ability to choose how you react. There's nothing forcing you to be reactive in your reactions, and as such, you always have the choice to be proactive, even in your responses.

So if you find yourself thinking, "It's because of him or her or that... that's why I ..." Stop. Acknowledge your ability to choose. And then shift the internal dialogue to: "I choose to (fill in the blank). Period."

90.

Just because you didn't do it the way you would
have liked to the time before doesn't mean you
won't make yourself proud this time. And just
because you were confused and not very sure
last time doesn't mean you won't have absolute
clarity this time.

Let last time be last time and this time be
this time.

91.

Close your eyes. Breathe. And then:
> *Thank you.*
> *Thank you.*
> *I'm so grateful that ...*
> Feel it. Mean it.

92.

No matter what kind of change you make —
whether you're adjusting your opinion,
revisiting your wants, or shifting your ways —
be sure that the goal isn't to change you, but
instead to become more of who you really are.

There's a reason certain changes feel off-
kilter and others resonate on every level.

93.

When your feelings get hurt, sometimes you decide to say nothing, because you don't want to suggest or confirm that someone has an effect on you, or admit that anything bothers you, or because you think it's your fault, but still, it nags at you. "Something isn't right. I can't ignore this," you keep hearing from a part of you.

Reach deep. Find the courage to say what you have to say while letting go of the results. It's not about what will happen next; it's about you saying your truth. That's all. That's everything. You're not giving your power away; you're taking it back.

It's one of the hardest yet most rewarding things to do: to admit someone matters to you enough that they have the capacity to hurt you. And that you matter enough to call it out.

And on the flip side, if someone ever tells you that they feel hurt by you, before you think of anything else, think about the fact that you matter that much to them.

94.

When you know you're wrong, admit it. When you realize you've gone too far, back down. But when your gut instinct tells you that you're right or that you're onto something, don't pretend you're probably wrong, and by all means don't retreat back into your shell, backing down. It's in those moments that you need to quiet any voices of doubt, whether coming from you or someone else, and push forward through to clarity.

Believe in yourself, trust what you know, listen to your gut instinct, and stick with your truth. Confidently and filled with hope.

95.

Ignoring the big, white elephant in the room
doesn't make it go away;
it just makes it bigger.

Acknowledge it and take a good look at it.

Call it as you see it.

Doing so puts it in perspective, making it
just part of the scenery.

96.

When you care about someone, the most important thing you can do for them doesn't come from your words or actions. It's in how you deliberately choose to think of that person every time they enter your mind.

Wherever they're at, no matter what's going on with them, hold them in the highest light in your mind, with all of their qualities shining through. Believe in them. Feel a deep trust in them—in their wisdom and in their ability to make choices for themselves. Envision them happy, even happier than you've ever seen them. Picture them at their best and then see them as even better than that.

97.

Never underestimate the power of your
directed and focused love.

It works miracles.

98.

There are key ingredients that make your life work, that make you feel alive and vibrant. They make you feel the magic, and they're particular to you. Along the way in life, lots of things can seem more important than those ingredients. Those other things can disguise themselves as priorities, and if you let them start to top your list, you might end up convincing yourself you're doing the right thing, the generous thing, what needs to be done.

Keep this in mind: the most generous thing you can do is be a role model for what it's like to live with vibrancy, to love your life while fully embracing your responsibilities and possibilities. It's sometimes a fine line, but you can walk it with finesse and love and consideration. You'll know what it is to be happy while not compromising someone else's happiness. You'll discover that the two have always been and will always be entwined because vibrancy is contagious.

99.

Things aren't always what they seem.
It's good to remember that.

100.

No matter what kind of relationship you have with someone, sometimes when you're trying to fix it or improve it, it can feel like you're running into a heavy barrier, like there's significant static standing in the way of things getting better. Despite what you try, nothing seems to be working, and some of your efforts can even feel like they're making things worse. When that happens, step off the track you've been on, be still for a moment, and ask yourself a powerful question: "How can I love them better?"

What would it look like? What would it feel like? Take your time. Think about it for as long as you want to...

Even just considering the question, you'll notice a palpable shift in the energy of the relationship.

And an interesting byproduct of the effort to love someone better is that you end up loving yourself better as well.

101.

The nicer you are to yourself, the nicer other people are to you.

And the happier you are to be you, the happier other people are to be around you.

And the more fun you think you are, the more fun you have and the more fun other people have with you.

102.

Notice that some of your biggest moments of
relief, some of your most rewarding moments
of honesty, and some of your happiest times
have coincided with a willingness to let your
flaws be seen, your imperfections noticed, your
doubts voiced, your fears admitted, and your
feelings spoken.

103.

It's easy enough to embrace all the things in your relationship that are working perfectly and look just the way you want them to, but what makes you feel vividly alive, surprisingly in control of your life, and happy to the point where some people might actually look at you strangely, is wrapping your arms around the raw, jagged-edged, far-from-perfect things in your relationship—simply because you're alive to experience them, right now, in this moment.

104.

Don't be afraid to completely change
your mind, surprising even yourself.

What happens next is usually as rewarding as
it is unpredictable.

105.

As well as you know those people closest to
you, and as much as you can infer about someone
you just met, keep in mind that the only person
whose full story-of-the-moment you can ever
know is your own.

When you approach an interaction with
as little judgment as you can and as much
curiosity as you can, good things happen.

106.

Your path is as individual as you are, and it's the perfect one for you. It's not always easy, but the obstacles you encounter and the hurdles you cross are there for a reason. They're part of your journey, and since the moment you were born and began this journey, you've had everything you've ever needed inside you to walk through the steeper terrains and bring yourself to the destinations you seek, time and time again.

The same is true for each person in your life. They too are on their own journey. So whether it's someone who walks right next to you or someone whose path is miles away, allow them their own internal space, explicitly trusting them and their journey.

107.

Go to that place of complete stillness inside
you, the place without words.

Close your eyes, breathe deeply, and relax
into that space within you.

In the silent stillness, you'll know whatever
it is you've wanted to know.

And you'll know you've allowed your own
wisdom to fully speak to you, in the way
that only it can, when you feel exactly how
you've been wanting to feel.

108.

If you continuously chase after a particular butterfly, you may find it flying away from you, constantly out of reach. But if you were to stop... and then pause your seeking for a moment... it might just turn around, fly to you, and land on your outstretched hand.

Or, another butterfly, one you hadn't even noticed, might finally have the opportunity to get your attention.

109.

You don't need to change.
You need only to love exactly who you are.
You don't need to change anyone else.
You need only to love exactly who they are.

110.

Never let fear of any kind get in the way of you standing up for yourself.

Sometimes it requires words, and sometimes silence. Sometimes action, and sometimes non-action. You always instinctively know.

You count. You matter. Show it.

It's interesting. The more willing you are to readily stand up for yourself, the less you end up needing to.

111.

You get to decide who you are.
All of it.

112.

You're never bound by your past experiences
or anyone else's version of what you should
expect.

Leave the idea that it has to be this way —
simply because it was once before — behind you,
and then step forward unencumbered.

Each day, each interaction is a new one.
Spilling over with possibilities.

113.

There are a lot of things you might accomplish today. You might finish a project, close a deal, cross something significant off a list. You might even come up with a great idea, have a breakthrough, take a step you've never taken. These are all important and good, and they matter a lot. But nothing—nothing—will shape your life personally and professionally or matter quite in the same way at the end of the day as you making even one person smile, inside and out.

One person. One smile that can be felt in every cell of that person's being.

When you affect one person, you affect everyone. Including yourself.

114.

Be curious. Get interested. Ask questions.
And...
Be open. Get real. Answer questions.

115.

You don't have to be in the same boat with someone for it to work—for you to get along beautifully and for you to experience a profound connection with each other. In fact, you can each be in your own boat, one rowing and one hoisting a sail, one moving faster today and slower tomorrow, one a little off-course yesterday and stopping to rest today.

What matters is that your boats are close enough for you to effectively communicate with each other and that, ultimately, you both want the same thing and are therefore making your way toward the same destination.

116.

Every relationship you have, no matter the circumstances or the level of commitment, is not only where you derive meaning, it's also a platform for you to express and become more of who you are. As such, it's important to step outside of that intermingling of energies once in a while, for a moment, and ask yourself, *Who am I without her? What do I look like without him in the picture?* It may look emptier at first, but the more you focus on the question, the more the different facets and characteristics of you will fill in the picture... until it's fuller than it was before.

Remember who you are on your own, what you look like separate from the people who matter the most to you. When you remember, you can be that person again, shape things again from scratch, and the people you're intermingled with can experience you being fully you again. What a gift.

117.

"How are you?" can be one of the most moment-
altering questions you ever ask, especially
when you ask it of yourself.

And the more often you ask yourself that
question and then go on to answer with total
honesty and openness, the more you realize the
enormous value of your friendship with you.

And the better you'll be at asking someone
else the question.

118.

Ask yourself what you need.

Then get still. Get quiet. And open up to
whatever the answer might be—
even if it's something you weren't expecting.

Now you know. And now you can do
something about it.

119.

Be who you are and let others be who they are. Accept responsibility for what's yours, whether it's your mood, what you need to get done, your way of thinking, or how you go about things. And let other people be responsible for what's theirs. There's no need to take on or let yourself be affected by what belongs to someone else; mixing the two benefits no one. Instead, peacefully and gratefully coexist side by side.

The clear separation is a beautiful thing.

120.

It's more than okay if you find yourself not knowing exactly what to say. And it's not a problem if your feelings are mixed. Don't worry if, at the moment, you're unsure of anything.

That's when you get to just show up. Simply arrive with the fullness of who you are. It doesn't require words. Or actions. Or anything else. It's so much bigger than that. It's a standing-still-in-the-moment, I'm-here-and-totally-present-with-you energy.

With no agenda.

Oh the lucky ones who get to experience you doing that.

121.

Your feelings deserve a voice, and you're the only one who can sing your song.

And when you do that, other people feel safe enough to sing their songs too.

122.

When someone's not doing well—either they're not feeling good, they're in a rut, they're frustrated about something and that frustration is taking over, or they're just plain down—you can react in one of two ways. You can get down on them for being down because of all the ways it affects you, or you can look at them and see something other than them not doing well.

You can look at them and choose to see, imagine, and feel the opposite. You can look at them and picture them feeling the best they've ever felt. You can envision them on top of their game. You can look at them and imagine them being excited and at peace, happy and fulfilled.

When you do that for someone, you play a huge role in getting them from down low to up where they belong. Just by seeing them there, believing in their ability to get there, and loving them on the way.

It feels good to play the role of a ladder.

123.

Wherever you're at is perfect.

124.

When you remember that the only variable you have control over in any relationship is you, it shows. You worry less, you need less, and you let go of more. Things get much clearer, much simpler.

And all those things that you want from the other person... when you focus on being those things yourself, cultivating them in you before looking for them in the other person, things get even clearer, even simpler.

And when your only goal is to be true to who you are, not to change who you are or who anyone else is, the relationship becomes a gift, and something simple suddenly becomes clear: it—all of it—is good. And so are you. And so are they.

125.

Make time for them.
That's how they know they matter.

126.

Take the time to express how you feel.

You don't have to keep your thoughts bottled inside, waiting for someone or something else to pop the cork so they can finally come bubbling out.

Go ahead and take on the role of cork-popper yourself. Expressing how you feel inevitably leads to some of the greatest discoveries, insights, and clarity you'll ever have. About everything... including and especially, how you really feel.

Take the time. Pop the cork.

127.

When something hurts, and it won't go away, it's going to be okay.

First, recognize that you're multidimensional, that there are countless facets of your being. And through that, you can recognize that a part of you is hurt, a very specific part rather than all of who you are. Then, call that hurt exactly what it is, avoiding the temptation to call it by any other name. And finally, acknowledge it by sitting with it and giving it the attention it deserves.

When you stop asking it to just go away, and you instead embrace it, it begins to heal.

128.

One of the greatest gifts you can give anyone
who means the world to you is to love yourself
unconditionally. Even though... and even
when... and especially when it's the last thing
you think you should be doing.

To love you — always, no matter what — is to
love them, always, no matter what.

129.

There are people who come into your life for a season, a decade, a lifetime. They're the ones with whom you walk, sometimes together, sometimes far apart, and on all kinds of terrain. Having them by your side, in any capacity and on any journey, allows you to see what you might not have otherwise seen when you look in the mirror.

And then there are people who come into your life for a moment, a blip, so quickly you're tempted to think it wasn't real, not nearly long enough to refer to, and yet, they affect you in a way that lasts. You have moment- and even life-changing conversations without a word ever spoken between you and a stranger. You can't forget them. And you wouldn't want to. Because they too pulled something out of the mirror that was never there before.

You're always noticing or being noticed; you're always teaching or being taught. And when you see that, it's hard to think of interacting with another person as anything other than an incredible gift. For you. For them.

130.

Discover a hundred ways
to be nice to them.

131.

It's a monumental, moment-changing decision when you choose to pause, take a deep breath (inhaling what you need, exhaling what you don't), and focus on the fact that everyone is doing the best they can.

Including you.

It's an unspoken, powerful reminder to the other person that they're not alone. And a reminder to yourself that neither are you.

It immediately opens the space for wisdom, empathy, understanding, confidence, bravery, and most importantly, honesty. Honesty connects you back to yourself and then opens up the possibility for a true connection with someone else.

It's an incredible gift. Love in one of its most extreme forms. Nothing less than a spiritual experience.

132.

There's absolutely nothing wrong with you.
Nothing.

There's nothing you are that you're not
supposed to be, and there's nothing you need
to be that you aren't already.

Grow, learn, and adapt,
but don't change you.

133.

Even with the best of intentions, criticizing other people never accomplishes its aim. No one ends up feeling better about themselves; in fact, the opposite ends up happening.

Imagine two people standing on the top two rungs of a ladder. The one criticizing is on the top rung, and with every criticism the person on the rung below internalizes, they both take a step down. The negativity doesn't just push the one being criticized down, it simultaneously pulls the one who's criticizing down as well, because in order to make sure the other person really "gets it," the one criticizing stays right there with them, forcing downward movement. Down another step they both go... until they're at the bottom, both silently left wondering, *What good did any of that do?*

Now imagine two people on the bottom two rungs of a ladder. The one on the very bottom compliments the person on the rung above. They move up a step together. In order to fully support the person trying to climb up to a better place, a better self-image, the person doing the complimenting continues to promise that they're right behind them, that they won't fall, that they can make it up another step. And so together, they move up and up and up.

134.

Refuse to dull any part of you. Express
yourself. Speak your truth. Be bold. Do your
thing. Trust yourself. Follow your instincts.
Feel how you feel.

Don't worry about what people might think or
how they'll react; if what you say and do comes
from the center of your authenticity, a place
your heart is always tapped into, it'll feel
right and good no matter what. And you'll see
the results of that.

The more authentic you are — true to yourself
and real — the bigger the outcome. Every time.

The most powerful course of action is
always, no matter what the scenario, for you to
be authentically you.

135.

Slow down...
Listen...

136.

An actor consciously chooses how to play out
each particular scene in the story of their
life, whether it's with no drama at all,
abundant ebullience, serious attention, a
quiet moment of silence, or a generous sense of
humor.

When someone chooses to be the reactor, on
the other hand, they often find themselves at
the mercy of all the choices the other actor
makes, and so they must constantly adjust
accordingly.

Empower yourself. Set the stage. Be the
actor, even when it's your turn to react.

137.

Two birds sat side-by-side having a discussion they'd had many times before. The second bird was explaining why it couldn't fly. It was just too difficult, it had never really been taught how to do it, it had tried and been unable to in the past. The list went on.

To each reason, the first bird had only one response. For the fourth time during their conversation, the first bird repeated, "I just can't picture you not flying; it doesn't jive with how I've always thought of you. I can only see you lifting your wings, letting the current of the wind carry you. I see you soaring, dipping and rolling with the changing skies, having a huge adventure of it, laughing, thrilled by the—" The bird stopped talking and smiled. It looked to the left and to the right, taking in all the details of the moment, and then joined the second bird, who was soaring in flight.

"Thank you," the second bird said when the first bird was at its side in midair. "Thank you for holding that vision of me when I couldn't hold it for myself."

And together they flew and flew and flew, so much higher and farther than either of them would've flown without the other.

138.

When you give someone a reason to laugh, you give them everything.

And when you laugh with them, it tells them everything they need to know: this moment is good, and you're not alone, and life is good, and none of us are alone.

May the laughter inside you and next to you overflow so much today and tonight that tomorrow you wake up laughing.

139.

Sometimes you have to look at the thorns simply because they're there, and when they come into play, it does no good to pretend they don't exist. In fact, by being aware of them and acknowledging them, you lessen the chance of being taken off guard and affected by their sharpness.

But the majority of the time, the thorns are just there, a necessary part of the flower as a whole. That's when it's important to see the petals. When you look at and talk about and focus on the petals, you infuse the flower with the energy to grow and bloom and be its vibrant self.

It's not possible to overestimate the power of your positive attention. When you give it, something happens. Every time.

140.

Nothing is more important than noticing when a
relationship you care about is starting to lose
its vibrancy — nothing except stopping what
you're in the middle of doing in order to do
something about it.

141.

Play together.

142.

By its very nature, when you contribute to
someone else's song, you create perfectly
resonating notes of your own. And the more
you do it, the more you find yourself leaning
into the music, becoming the vibration of
it — because it feels so good, so right, so
uplifting, so in tune with who you are.

143.

You can feel it, when you have an edge to you, when certain topics of conversation or specific triggers cause a tightening in you, a sharpness that defines your perspective in that moment, your voice, your actions.

Sharp edges tend to be painful on a number of levels. So pause and take the necessary time to soften that edge. The edge is a result of you bumping up against something that's adamant about needing your attention. So then, the most obvious way to soften that edge is to simply give it your attention. What's the edge saying to you? By allowing the edge to tell you what it's been trying to tell you, the edge softens, calms down. You can then respond to what the edge told you, which almost always means giving yourself what you need.

That edge was just trying to let you know that what you need is important.

144.

"I love you."

The power of those three words
can alter what you see, dissolve what doesn't
belong in the picture, and
shape-shift an entire situation.

Whether you say it to yourself
or to someone else.

Try it, especially when you most doubt
it will work.

145.

It can be helpful to recognize that when someone's not happy, their way of being tends to challenge happiness in general—the possibility of it, the validity of it, its longevity when it exists, and the wherewithal of other people's happiness.

And it can be helpful to recognize that when someone's committed to being happy no matter what, their way of being tends to confirm the possibility of happiness, validate other people's experience of it, remove the question of its longevity, and contribute to the creation of it.

See clearly, your eyes open to simply what is.

146.

In every relationship, you and the other person act out scenes together, one after another, to eventually create an entire story.

No matter what the scene is or who it's with, you always have two choices.

You can keep rolling with the scene because it's working, flowing, and together you're acting out something you like.

Or you can say "cut," step away for a moment, and then come back after having decided on your new role.

147.

When you suddenly stop and remember that
it's about certain people — that in the end,
those particular people in your life and your
interactions with them are all that really
matter — something changes in you.

Something simple. Something beautiful.

You look like you're listening to the best
song ever written, recognizing it, for the
first time, as your own.

148.

Look at someone — anyone — and just see what you
see. (It takes a second.)

Then look deeper, past the obvious. (It takes
about three seconds.)

And then even further, to where it's not
about anything that can actually be seen.
(Time will be irrelevant.)

No matter who you decide to really look at,
what you'll see will dramatically shift your
perspective and give you total clarity about
what really matters.

149.

As a child, you had it mastered. You have it in you now, it's still there—the ability to easily laugh, easily cry, easily understand, easily question, easily wonder, easily be, and easily connect. It's the art of having no agenda.

Put yourself in the same room as someone, or sit down with someone, or take a walk with someone. And then, choosing to give your time to that person, engage without any agenda—with no needs, with a willingness to let the other person direct the interaction, to steer whatever conversation may or may not take place. Go along for the ride, with no expectations, your only desire being to simply be with that person, to really see them and hear them and notice them and enjoy their presence.

Even if it ends up being just five minutes and not a word is spoken and nothing significant seems to happen, you'll profusely thank yourself afterwards for making the most important, best decision of your entire day.

150.

When you care about someone, the most powerful thing you can do for them is to hold them up in their highest light. Picture them having moved out of any darkness, life's energy wholly supporting them. Picture them at peace, excited, coming into the fullness of who they are.

When you change your thoughts about someone—determined to hold them up in their highest light, no matter what—it's a deep, effective act of caring.

151.

It's easy to assume you know someone and what
to expect from them. What's a challenge, a lot
more fun, and in everyone's best interest is
for you to let them pleasantly surprise you.
To open the space for them to throw you for a
loop and awe you. Because if you let them, they
will.

Give them more than just the benefit of the
doubt. Wildly believe in them.

The same goes for you. Pleasantly surprise
yourself. Awe you. Believe you can, and that's
exactly what you'll do.

152.

Every time you pause and say to yourself, "I like me. A lot," it shows, and you give a gift—one that's particular to each recipient.

For some people, you may be giving the gift of "It's okay for you to feel however you feel about me, because I've got it under control on my end."

For others, you may be giving the gift of "Yes, even in the confused, dark, and not so attractive moments, you can still love yourself. I do it all the time."

And still for others, you may be giving the gift of "Every aspect of your life becomes that much more fun and works that much better when you fully embrace the person at the center of it all."

Each time, you start a ripple effect, the kind that changes people's lives, including your own. Just by being contagiously happy to be you.

153.

Tell your stories. Tell them however they
move through you, in whatever form they take.
Because they matter.

Live your stories, share them, and then,
when other people are offering you their
stories to experience, you'll willingly
jump right into the adventure of it all,
understanding how you have the pcwer to
shape and to be shaped.

154.

You have the potential to have turning-point conversations every day, because being a good listener, a really good listener, can change someone's life.

And when it's your turn to talk, being authentic and courageously speaking your truth can change a life too.

It happens in conversations with both five-year-olds and ninety-five-year-olds, in conversations with those you've known forever and those you've just met. It starts out simply. A simple noticing. A simple observation. A simple expression of what is. A simple realization. A simple wondering. Every monumental shift was once a simple introduction into someone's consciousness.

155.

Be present. Fully show up.

Listen closely. Speak honestly.

The rest is magical.

156.

In order to live out your life in a way that's true to who you are and wholly meaningful, you need to have a clear sense of self.

All the people in your life provide a generous and ideal platform for you to continually discover and strengthen your sense of self, yet this can only be done if you consciously, gently extricate yourself from the entanglements and merging that naturally occur.

Challenge each other, love each other, grow because of each other, agree and disagree with each other, engage and inspire, entertain and be entertained... but always remain you, and allow them to be them.

157.

Asking yourself "What do I want?' is important.
But if you ever want to get what it is you
really want a little faster, ask yourself this
question: "How do I want to feel?" That's what
the answer to "What do I want?" is really all
about.

How do you want to feel?

There's no right or wrong answer. It's
simply a decision you make, and your awareness
of that decision is the key. Decide how you
want to feel, and you'll immediately begin
creating the kind of experiences that ignite
those feelings.

158.

If you're going to choose one rule to follow,
let it be this: never lie to yourself.

Honesty is a simple, direct path to love:
To a self-love permeating with peace. To
a love for someone else so complete in its
existence that it needs nothing. To a growing
love for your life that keeps expanding in new
directions.

159.

Call it like it is.
It's the difference between knowing you're
free and actually experiencing freedom.

160.

Resisting seeing what you see, trying not to hear what you hear, or pretending not to feel what you feel takes a lot of effort and energy and makes that which is being resisted so much bigger than it actually is. And it's exhausting.

Take your power back. You never have to hide from anything. See what you see, hear what you hear, and feel what you feel, letting it be what it is. Watch as what you were resisting then shrinks in size and power because instead of being afraid of it, you're standing up to it, owning it, facing it.

See how much smaller it is than you? It's tiny.

161.

If you're trying to muscle your way through sad
or angry or confused feelings, trying to hurry
it all up so you can get to a better place, be
gentle with you.

Take your time.

Feel what there is to feel.

And consider this: You won't feel better
until you're ready to. No matter what you do.
And that's not a bad thing.

162.

Love. Peace. Light.

Love. Peace. Light.

Love. Peace. Light.

There is no relationship that's not made better—even better or much, much better—by concentrating on those three words.

163.

Rather than taking a running leap and jumping to a conclusion, hold off, take a breather, and simply observe for a little while.

Interesting things tend to happen when you do that. Little details and nuances suddenly become apparent, one by one. Eventually, conclusions you hadn't thought of or considered meander along until they're standing right in front of you, impossible not to see.

Once in a while, detach and observe. You'll sometimes find what you least expected to see but always hoped to.

164.

You could be in the same room or hundreds of miles away from the person. It doesn't matter. Anytime you want to, you can let them know that you're grateful to them, that you believe in them, that you trust them, that it's going to be okay, that you're sorry, that you adore them... that they matter to you.

Think it. Feel it. Send it.

They'll receive it. They may not know where it came from. They may not know who it came from or why, but they'll instantly and immensely benefit from your energetic expression of love.

165.

Tell the story that's yours—regardless of
how it plays out in anyone else's book—
because the more you validate yourself, the
less validation you need and the more you
have to give. And that's the epitome of
empowerment.

166.

It can be scary to go to the bottom of the barrel of your thoughts and feelings, to admit those "What? Not me" things you're thinking and feeling. First, it doesn't sound like a fun place to go. Second, there's the concern of not being able to get out of what appears from a distance to be a dark, confining space. But here's the thing. If you're experiencing uneasy thoughts and feelings on any level, it's not fun anyway. And until you go there willingly, you're confining yourself in darkness unwittingly.

So how do you go to the bottom of the barrel? Take some time for you, and write, say, or draw whatever feelings are beneath all the others. It might take you days, but it could also take you just four minutes. In the end, you'll be saving so much time and energy, because going there is so much faster and more comfortable than the experience of fearing going there. Is it fun once you're there? No. It's exhilarating and immediately rewarding. Will you get stuck there? Absolutely not. You get out the same way you got in, because you choose to.

Be strong. Be you. Dig deep, and when you climb out, you'll be fearless and free and ready for what's next.

167.

Wonder how things could get even better,
and they will.

168.

Strive for authenticity in everything you do, but especially in what matters most to you.

There's a rawness to authenticity that can't be faked, and there's a realness to it that can't be duplicated by anyone else.

It's your truth, pulled from a place deep inside you that isn't concerned with being judged or criticized or praised. It asks for nothing. It needs nothing. Except to be expressed.

It's your greatest asset, inherent in your greatest talents. It's your greatest gift to give, and the results of doing so, of being completely real, will never cease to astound you.

Authenticity is what distinctively sets you apart when standing out isn't even on your radar.

169.

Love is one of those circular phenomena. As much as it's a catalyst, a motivator, and the best reason ever, it's also always part of the answer and every solution.

Love as if simply doing so will miraculously solve any dilemma, repair what needs to be fixed, and heal whatever is broken. And it will.

When you want to know what the point of something is or why something's happening, give it all the love you have to give. And then you'll know.

When you want to understand yourself or someone else better... love, love, love. And you'll totally understand.

Love like it's all that really matters. And then it will be.

170.

It's important to take the time to process things on your own, to think things through, to feel them out for yourself, to figure out where you're at.

But then at some point—and you always know when that point is—it becomes necessary to talk about things out loud: to voice your opinion, declare your thoughts, engage in conversation, state your feelings, discover more about where you're at.

An energetic shift takes place when you say things out loud to someone, a movement from possibly to really, from maybe to more likely, bringing to life words that had once just been thoughts.

171.

Sometimes the answer is to just let go — to
free them, to free you.

By letting go, you realize what it was you
were really trying to hold on to, and that it,
what it actually was, is still cradled securely
in your grasp.

172.

The plumeria is a wildly vibrant, exotic plant. But if you cut the flowers from the stem, the petals immediately start to wither.

In the stem is all that makes the plumeria happy, all that the plumeria needs to thrive.

Make a point of always knowing what your stem consists of.

173.

There's nothing that isn't made better
by your sense of humor
and taking whatever it is
a little less seriously.

174.

Be kind.

However you can—always.

Whenever you can—always.

It's the simple things that define
and shape a relationship.

175.

There are times between those of active doing that call for sitting still and absorbing the here and now. In those moments, slow, deep breaths allow you to look closer and gaze longer. In those moments, your own silence lets you hear more and listen in a way you haven't.

The magic in those moments is tangible; you can feel it, even see it in the space between you and everything, around you and everything. A patience blankets the moment, surrounding you and your world in loving arms, soothing, calming, assuring. And it becomes not only possible but absolute that in those moments you see and hear in the varied languages of your soul that everything is exactly as it needs to be, that everything is in motion, and that you can rest, really rest, assured that everything is working out even better than you imagined during all the times of active doing.

Relax into the moment of now, allowing it to present you with all its gifts.

176.

Stop and ask yourself, "What am I doing?"

The answer can surprise you and sometimes even take you by the hand and lead you from now to next.

177.

There will be times when you'll know something isn't working or isn't how you want it to be, but you won't know what to do. What you'll have tried won't have worked, and you'll come to the point where you've run out of ideas and the whole thing's starting to weigh a little too much.

It's okay. It's really okay.

When that happens, let go and do nothing. Just sit still and gently observe. With an open mind and an open heart, let things be as they are.

It's working itself out, and at the perfect time, you'll know exactly what to do.

178.

Let go of the need to be right.
And feel the thrill of holding hands
with life's pulse.

179.

At any point, you can stop what you're in the middle of doing. You can turn off the thoughts you've been thinking. You can pause in the midst of what you were saying.

Each moment of now is a blank canvas. You can do with it as you choose.

The words you speak will paint the scenery, filling in colors accordingly.

Your beliefs in any moment—they determine the mood of the sky.

Your action—what you choose to do with this moment—will lead you to what's next, something not yet determined, not until you decide.

The possibilities for your relationships are endless. This moment is yours. It's a gift. A right. An honor. What will you do with it?

180.

Think about how many times a day you wonder, and how many things you wonder about over the course of a day...

Whenever you wonder, assume the best.

The very, very best.

You'll be glad you did.

181.

When you're authentically you, people know it,
and they love it, because it's a silent nod of
encouragement from you, one that says, "Yes, go
ahead and be yourself too."

182.

Your presence alone has the power to heal
and the strength to create.

Remember that.

183.

When you talk like you and act like you, it's such a good feeling—no matter what the conversation is about.

In the midst of a conversation, there isn't a lot of space to think it through—am I being me? Which is perfect, because it's not something you can think through. You feel your way to it. You can tell if you've put on a mask, adopted someone else's ways for the moment, or are saying something that's bending further and further from who you really are. You can feel it.

When you're you, you're like a firmly rooted tree. Your branches sway in the wind, adjusting as necessary but always stemming from the strength of your core. Your leaves are your own, and the wind whistles a song through them that's like no other.

You can decide, in any moment, in the middle of any conversation, that you have one priority right then: to be you. That's it.

184.

Tap into your strength—the roar inside you that stands up for itself, the discernment that allows you to see what you want and what you don't want, to know what you'll put up with and what you won't.

Tap into the strength you have to let go when it's necessary and hold on when you need to. Tap into the strength you have to go with the flow when in a current and switch directions when it's time to.

Your trust, your confidence, your optimism, and your laughter, they're all born from a deep well of strength within you. Your ability to wait with patience, to boldly step forward when it's time, they also come from that deep well of strength.

By tapping into that well of strength, you unleash your will power, your wisdom, your capacity for joy, and your creativity. And when tapping into your strength, you find out who you really are and what love actually means.

There is no end to—and no relationship that doesn't benefit from—the deep well of strength inside you.

185.

Go out of your way to be nice.
Just because.

186.

Like a master potter holding a ball of clay, you can mold any moment and any situation into anything you want it to be. You can round it out, pound it in, soften the edges, spin it in any direction, form it into something useful... even change your mind, ball it back up, and start all over again.

And in doing so, you define your role.

Like an artist's signature, you always, always leave your mark. Leave it with gusto, and love what you leave.

187.

You're good enough.
And you're completely worthy
and fully deserving.
Question a lot of things but never that.

188.

Take your time and gift it to them,
giving them your undivided attention.

189.

Keep discovering you're way stronger,
much wiser, and a lot more fun than
you thought you were.
Keep discovering you.

190.

It's not always easy to say what you think and express how you feel. But it's important, because what you think matters, as does how you feel.

There's no one here but you to contribute your individual perspective, wherever it is you're coming from. Sometimes it's the simplest words—what you might even consider the least consequential thing to say—that end up turning the tide, or being the perfect challenge, or giving a comfort more necessary than you'll ever be aware of. You're there, wherever you are, among the people you're with, for a reason: to contribute what you can, to say what you will, to share who you are.

Give of you—what you think and how you feel—the most consequential thing there is to give.

191.

It's not a contest.

Just be the best you can be.

192.

If you try to please too many people, you'll end up with a watered-down version of what you're capable of.

Aim to let whatever you do — no matter what it is — represent you, nothing held back. Give what you do your all. Get raw and commit to real. It changes the entire energy of what you put out there.

And it changes your relationships.

Don't worry about how it looks or what it might sound like. Make no assumptions about what people will think, because it doesn't matter. Give your attention to simply making sure it fully represents you. And then bask in that feeling — and in that accomplishment.

No one else can offer what you have to give, no matter what it is.

193.

You are love, and that's why every expression of it you offer—even a simple one—resonates so strongly, giving you instantaneous peace, making you feel whole and complete.

You are love. That's why every time you check in with yourself, with who you truly are, and then speak or act standing firmly in a place of love, it lifts your spirit, sending it soaring where it knows it belongs.

You are love. When you look at someone or something with that knowing—I am love—you can't help but see it everywhere else too. You see love in every person and place and situation, in every crevice and corner, and you have no doubt that it's all good, it's all working out.

You are love, and so when you tap into that knowing, your power comes back to you, and your confidence has no reason to do anything but increase and carry you where your heart directs you.

You are love. In the beginning and the end, that's all you need to remember.

If you enjoyed Notes from Gusto,
please consider posting a review at Amazon
or elsewhere online.

Thank you!

Also by Elizabeth Day:

Living with Gusto
A Novel

Notes from Gusto: Break Free

You're Invited

Hang out with Gusto at TheGustoCafe.com.

TheGustoCafe.com is open 24/7, with the exact love note you need, whenever you need it—because you're awesome, and it's important to remember that.

Explore the café and find powerful Relationship Reminders, helpful Timing Tips, and daily Power Thoughts. Read a page in the Empowerment Diary and feel your confidence soar. Get encouraged and excited by reading a Note to You from Your Future Self. Listen to music and read a short, moving Love Story. Get advice about how to interact with money and learn how to live your dream—today, right now. Post your thoughts and be heard. Click on the ladder in the café and climb out of any rut. Click on the wall art in the café and get inspired to fall even more in love with your life.

Get wildly empowered.

Hang out with Gusto at TheGustoCafe.com.

About the Author

Elizabeth Day lives in San Clemente, California, and Todos Santos, Mexico, with her husband and two children.